Seasoning the Soul

Second Edition

Meditations for the Celtic Year

Collected and edited by Eileen Knoff, D.Min.

Seasoning the Soul
Second Edition
Meditations for the Celtic Year

Collected and edited by Eileen Knoff, D.Min.

Published by Pilgrim Spirit Communications
Tacoma, Washington
2018

ISBN 978-0-692-97207-6

All rights reserved.

No part of this book may be used or reproduced in any manner whatsoever without written permission of the editor, as well as the author, photographer, illustrator, or other entity involved in the section in question. Rights to reproduce a part of the book are reserved to the original contributor(s) of those works.

Many, though not all, of the works included here were first published as part of a monthly publication called *Brigid's Circle* prepared and distributed by email to subscribers between 2008 and 2012 under the auspices of Spiritual Directions, LLC. All material included here has been used with permission of the original creators.

Originally published in 2012 (Revised 2016) as
Seasoning the Soul: Images and Reflections with a Celtic Flavor to Bless Your Year
Published by Spiritual Directions, LLC.
Redmond, Washington

Cover photo copyright 2012 Liz Knoff Floodeen

I dedicate this second edition to the four females
who have most influenced my becoming the woman I am today~

My mother, Grace McLaughlin Loeher (1918-2003)
My sister, Kathleen Loeher Bonneau
My daughter, Elizabeth Knoff Floodeen
and my granddaughter, Aria Grace Floodeen.

Contents

Introduction 1

The Season of Samhain (Winter) 9
Entering Winter 10
Dwelling in Winter 18
Releasing Winter 24
Questions for Reflection by Individuals or Groups 30

The Season of Imbolc (Spring) 35
Entering Spring 36
Dwelling in Spring 40
Releasing Spring 52
Questions for Reflection by Individuals or Groups 58

The Season of Beltane (Summer) 61
Entering Summer 62
Dwelling in Summer 68
Releasing Summer 80
Questions for Reflection by Individuals or Groups 88

The Season of Lughnasadh (Autumn) 91
Entering Autumn 92
Dwelling in Autumn 98
Releasing Autumn 104
Questions for Reflection by Individuals or Groups 116
Annotated Bibliography 119

Index of Contributors 127
Personal Reflections 129

Come,
you who travel through time,

back to an ancient way
and across a threshold
into the year
ahead.

May companions of your soul
comfort you in offering keys
to unlock Mystery
in each moment:
a focused eye, well-tuned ear,
subtle tongue and gentle touch.

Come, let Earth tell
Her age-old secrets.

Come, travel to that space
where light arises from the dark recesses
of your pilgrim heart.

Each pilgrim tells a different tale.
What will you relate
when you return from the year ahead?

~ Eileen Knoff

Prayer to the Muse

I seek you in all I do
that I don't miss red
on the winging blackbird,
or the green leaf sprouting
after winter's chill.

~ Jan Phillips in *Marry Your Muse*

Introduction

A warm welcome to the second edition of Seasoning the Soul

This collection of poems, prayers, essays, and photographs reflects life through the rhythm of the seasons and the lens of Celtic spirituality. This classic spirituality with roots hundreds of years before Christ has left its trace on cultures across Europe even as it continues to attract adherents today from all over the world.

Perhaps Celtic spirituality's long and vibrant life is due to its zest for weaving together what can be seen, tasted, heard, touched, and smelled with a sensitivity to what lies just beyond the tangible. Perhaps it is the way the Celtic view embraces the present moment as it sets out to explore the unknown ahead. Perhaps its longevity lies in being grounded in Gaelic lands and language while stretching its arms to all of humanity.

There is something in the spirituality too true to be tamed by any one group.

This truth lies, I believe, in its core values, as described by the *Solas Bhride* website (solasbhride.ie), a site run by the Sisters of St. Brigid of Kildare. These values appeal to a wide cross section of people. Celtic spirituality includes a love of the earth, a welcome for the stranger, a sense of the sacred in all creation, a place for pilgrimage and prayer, an appreciation of solitude and silence, a eagerness to bless the ordinary tasks of life, and a tradition of having soul friends with whom to journey through life.

The contributors to this book have been soul friends on my journey through life. I dearly hope they will become your soul friends as well and that these Celtic spiritual values will shine through their words and images on these pages.

Who is likely to enjoy this book

Seasoning the Soul can be enjoyed by anyone who values taking time periodically to contemplate life and spend time in the beauty of nature. It is for those curious about the Celtic spiritual perspective as well as those who know it and want to live more fully into it. It is for those who want to embrace the gifts offered by each season of the year and each season of our lives.

I hope this book will also prove attractive to teachers and students of inter-spirituality—a growing movement that values persons listening deeply to one another's experiences of the sacred no matter their respective faith or cultural backgrounds. Inter-spirituality is something like a jewel with many facets, each facet's reflection of Light being equally valuable and all contributing to the luminosity of the gem as a whole. This book is like that gem with each entry one of the facets, offering vital light and beauty to the whole. Entries come from the experiences of two dozen women and men of diverse spiritual perspectives. Some are Catholic, some would call themselves Progressive Christians, some prefer to be called simply contemplative, some declare no preference, at least one is Unitarian, and another agnostic. Some lean more toward a naturalistic Celtic spirituality, others toward a more Christian one.

This book does seek to cross bridges of belief and serve as a bridge into a new kind of spiritual future where we can all appreciate the diverse ways in which the Sacred reveals itself through and to humanity. If you see yourself as seeking to explore that future, you will likely enjoy this book.

What you will find in this second edition

The same reflections and photographs that so appealed to the readers and reviewers of the first edition serve as the core content of this book as well. They invite you now—as they did then—to enter into each season, dwell there, and release the season to make way for the new.

I have stayed with naming the seasons with the ancient Celtic terms, beginning with *Samhain*, meaning *summer's end*, which starts November 1 as days grow darker, seeds and bulbs settle into the earth to wait in darkness for emergence in Spring (*Imbolc*), February 1. This is the time when animals start to give birth and lactate; new buds begin to peek out of the ground. May 1 celebrates the start of Summer (*Beltane*) which comes to its climax in late June and early July and then begins to slide into the time of first fruits, *Lughnasadh*, August 1. These starting dates are called *cross-quarter days* because they happen halfway between the solstices and equinoxes, the days Western culture starts the seasons. On these cross-quarter days you may see hints of seasonal change if you look closely. Light may shine just a bit more brightly or glow more softly than in the days behind. There may be a new chill in the air or a slight warming. Animals come out of hiding or go into it. Ice may begin to melt; rains may start to fall.

Preface

The more I have let myself be influenced over the years by this Celtic calendar, the more my senses have been sharpened to notice small changes—not only in the earth but also in myself and in other people. I have learned to pay better attention to what is emerging in my life and to live that cycle of emergence, fullness, and letting go with greater acceptance. I suspect you'll notice similar changes happening in you if you let a Celtic perspective on the seasons settle into your soul.

You will be introduced to the god Lugh, a Celtic god of light, and the goddess Brigid, known as a goddess of fire, poetry, and fertility among other things. In Celtic Christianity she stands with Patrick and Columba as one of the three most highly respected saints of Ireland. She is said to have led a monastery of women and men in the 5th century in Kildare and was known for her leadership, compassion, and complete devotion of the Divine. She was ordained into her leadership over the protests of some when her bishops said it was by the Holy Spirit's insistence that he was blessing Brigid's leadership. Her followers have kept her flame lit for centuries. Where the goddess Brigid ends and the saint begins is a very blurred line.

In either world Brigid carries a sense of the Sacred as imaged in woman. In that regard she offers a helpful corrective to how our human language for the divine has been heavily weighted toward the masculine. Some would say, and I am among them, weighted too heavily toward the masculine. Whenever one image of God predominates such that it excludes all other images of the Sacred it becomes an idol and our understanding of God is contorted. Hence you will find in these pages diverse ways of imaging the sacred—ways from the feminine, the masculine, and from nature. Such a multi-form way of imaging God can be a source of human liberation. It is my hope that the inclusive imaging of the holy in this book will help you experience a revelation of the mystery that is God.

You will find at the end of this book a reference list on Celtic spirituality reflecting sources I have found helpful. I realize there is a long and rich tradition of the study of the Celts, their language, their mythology, their literature, their beliefs in both the pre-Christian and Christian cultures. This list barely scratches the surface. But it is a start and it does offer to you insight into sources that led through some of my personal studies into the spirituality.

A bit of background

The content of this book first saw the light of day between 2008 and 2011, when friends with a common interest in Celtic spirituality began to share emails online. As our connection grew more intentional we deepened our exploration of this spirituality through a monthly newsletter comprised of original essays, poetry, prayers, and photographs inspired by our interest in this spirituality. We started with five persons and grew to fifty by way of a bulk email process and subscribers willing to support the process financially. Nearly half the participants contributed a writing or photograph sometime over the course of our online connection. These writings and images form the basis for this book.

As time went on, I saw a value in preserving in more permanent form the wonderful wisdom and beauty of the monthly online contributions. I began to collect them and sought permissions from their creators to publish them in a book. In 2012 the first edition of this book, *Seasoning the Soul: Images and Reflections with a Celtic Flavor to Bless Your Year*, was born. Around that time, social media platforms came on the scene. Our group moved to Facebook where we discovered new tools to repost words and images of others who inspired us as well as our own. We continue today as a Facebook group.

If after reading this book you find yourself interested in participating in our group, please email me at eileenknoff@yahoo.com for more information on how to do that.

Over the years since publications readers of the first edition have shared their feedback with me. They have called the book *a rich spiritual resource, a fresh voice, a wonderful book that will speak to your soul*. They discovered within these pages *a feast for the eyes, heart-moving poetry, an accessible way of seeing the Sacred in the seemingly ordinary sights and events of our daily life*.

Because of this kind of response—other stories people told me of how it had given them hope during times of struggle—I decided to try to keep this book alive in a second edition when I found it necessary to dissolve Spiritual Directions LLC, its initial publisher. Technical editor and print coordinator Judith Jones, of Tacoma, Washington, was a crucial support in this effort. She has been a true believer in this book, reassuring me of its value whenever I started to question whether to keep it in print. She has assisted me all along the way in bringing this out again under the publishing guidance of Pilgrim Spirit Communications. Thank you, Judy, so very much.

How to read this book

Please do read this book in whatever way you most need too. If you purchase it before the start of the Celtic Year (November 1) you may decide to read it through from beginning to end and cover the entire Celtic year, from November 1-October 31. Or you might purchase it somewhere in between and pick it up there and start to read from whichever season you find yourself in at the time. You might want to read it alone, or as part of a group.

You might prefer to follow the external season that fits with how you are feeling internally. If you are in a darker emotional time of life, a time of waiting you may prefer the Samhain readings. If you are starting to embark on new opportunities or new directions you may find the Imbolc (spring) readings more fitting. If you are in a time of pausing to reflect on and collect your own experiences you may want to read more in the Lughnasdh period (autumn). You may be celebrating a time of abundance and want to focus on what you find in Beltane (summer).

One helpful way to enter into any kind of reflective reading is that of allowing yourself to let words or images or ideas or emotions that come to you simply simmer for a while. Be with them and allow them to take shape slowly. You might want to write about arises in a journal. You might want to go outside, take photographs, paint, play music, dance, or whatever creative activity best fits for you.

As I completed the final edit of the first edition I sensed a call to go outside. And so I did, down toward a pond that lies just beyond my backyard patio. I took photographs of the pond. I began to watch closely what lived on it and around it. I noticed its changes. That pond has since become the focus of new collection of poems. It was important that I listened to what I heard while reading this book to find what was next for me. If this book helps you find your way to what's next for you, I will consider it to have been highly successful.

Reflection questions at the end of each section can be fruitful for taking you further into your reflection or toward your next creative action. They also can serve to support the use of the book by groups whose members gather for spiritual support of one another.

What next

If after spending time with these reflections you find yourself desiring to learn more about the online group Brigid's Circle from which they emerged, please feel free to contact me at eileenknoff@yahoo.com. You can also find links related to the book on the website for Pilgrim Spirit Communication and www.seasoningthesoul.blogspot.com. As of the printing of this second edition I am still offering a bit of personal spiritual companioning. If you would like to explore that possibility with me, you can contact me at the yahoo email address shown above as well.

I deeply hope this book helps you to pause and notice what Life is offering to you in this present season. I do pray that you may be receptive to what that is and that it may help you open yourself to living Life to the Full.

May the Light of Life bless you, and bless you kindly.

Eileen Knoff, D.Min,
Redmond, Washington
September 1, 2017

Welcoming

Sing hallelujah
for the gift is here:

here in the breathing
here in the groaning
here in the birthing
here in the wondering

Sing praise and
with a joyful heart
welcome the gift
in each now moment.

~ Sharon Taylor

Photo by Barbie Hull Photography

SEASONING THE SOUL

Photo by Barbie Hull Photography

O Wisdom of Winter's Breath,
We pray, lead Us in Your Will and Way,
through lengthening night and diminishing light~

Present in the Deeper Sight of Season.

~ Cheryl Anne

The Season of Samhain (Winter)

All creatures have been drawn from nothingness.
> *~ Meister Eckhart*

Entering Winter

The Blessing of Samhain

May the darkness of the New Year
be your invitation for the pause we all need.

The chill in the air beckons
to look toward the veil ever so thin now
between us
and those who have gone before.

The New Year comes and blesses all
with reminders that their presence
is oh, so very close,
surrounding us with prayers.

Winter approaches, Samhain is its song.
There is a distinctive calling now,
Slow down, reflect, stay alert
for they are here.

~ Scott Jenkins

Photo by Stephen Knoff

About Samhain

The season of Samhain (pronounced Sow'in) means "summer's end." Samhain is a marker for the threshold point, or doorway, between the two primary phases of the Celtic year: the light phase of summer and the darker phase of winter. Some consider the point of Samhain to be the most significant of the Celtic seasons since it marks the start of the Celtic year and sets the year's cycle in motion. The Celts understood that "in dark silence come whisperings of new beginnings, the stirring of the seed below the ground."[1]

Samhain served as the primary transitional moment in the Celtic year. This point of shift between the seasons of light and dark was believed to be particularly *thin*—that is, a time when one could hope to connect with the unseen, invisible world from this tangible one. The connections often sought during these days were with those closest friends and relatives who had recently passed on in death, or with those men and women of inspiring stature, the more formal saints.

Photo by Diane Ahern Photography

---

[1] See www.chalicecentre.net/samhain.htm for more detailed information on Samhain. To explore possible connections between the ancient Celtic way of viewing the seasons and newer understandings of our evolving and unfolding universe, I suggest Diarmuid O'Murchu's *Evolutionary Faith* (Maryknoll, New York: Orbis Books, 2002), especially Chapter Three, "The Emptiness that Overflows." When cosmologists today write of a fecund emptiness in the quantum vacuum, I hear echoes of the Celts' poetic insight that from the darkness and emptiness of winter flows the new life of spring. Closely related to both of these is the Christian wisdom of The Paschal Mystery.

SEASONING THE SOUL

Our current Christian liturgical calendar reflects this same human desire to remember and connect with inspiring and beloved ancestors as we step into the future. The three-day sequence of All Hallows Eve (October 31), All Saints (November 1) and All Souls Days (November 2) offers us just that opportunity.

Today the All Hallows, All Saints, and All Souls triad encourages us to retain a sense of connection with those we love and admire whether we experience them physically with us or not. Like the interweaving of the Celtic knot, these transitional days between the old year and the new invite us to trust that life here and life beyond remain inextricably linked.

~ Eileen Knoff

Photo by Diane Ahern Photography

The Passing of Soul

On October 2, feast of the Guardian Angels, my Uncle Lavirtus died. He was a kind, gentle soul with a wonderful sense of humor. He lived a full life and made conscious choices about his dying. By all accounts, his passing was a beautiful and blessed death. What remains poignant now, when reflecting back on this experience, is that this death was the first time in my 57 years wherein upon learning of the impending passing of someone close to me, I felt joy.

His passing had been anticipated for the two weeks prior. Hospice had set up a bed in the family room, appropriately named for that is where his immediate family sat vigil. It was also where the rest of my family made pilgrimage in order to see him off. In the weeks before, I had been experiencing a heightened sense of the nearness of my grandparents. So when I received the news about my uncle, I understood that they were letting me know that all was prepared. They, too, were anticipating his passing.

As I sat with my uncle near the head of his hospice bed, I became aware of the expansiveness that resides in the present. In that moment, I experienced a depth of understanding of the affirmation, *all is in Divine order, all is well,* that escapes me at other times. Now, in the days following his funeral and celebration of life, one question lingers:

What part of my life needs to die so that, like Lazarus, I may be called into new light and life?
~ Sharon Taylor

Yes, darkness moves toward us. . . . It is good to believe
in the power of darkness, moist darkness, to prepare the way.

~ Sheila Dierks

Photo by Eileen Knoff

Words of Blessing

May this time of waiting be restful,
for you to hear your heart's desire.

May this time be graceful,
for you to continue to find newness in God.

May this time be open for you,
to grow into a new fullness and

bring to life all the love you hold.

~ from Michelle Conklin's *The Waiting and the Arrival*

Entering Winter

This month an abundance of beauty and nourishment graces our tables and calls forth gratitude for seeds planted in spring and cared for under the summer sun. That sun has morphed now into dark gray clouds which beckon me toward reflection.

I find myself looking back on my ancestors who planted the seeds that grew into me. I recognize their courage in passing through gates into the unknown. They offered a path for me to follow, yet left me free to choose my own way. . . . I wonder about what I have become.

What has been produced in me from others' efforts and my choices? What has not taken root? How have I walled off the garden that is my life today? How have I kept the gate open to welcome others?

. . . I bless the gift of winter, grateful for the time it leaves me to look deeper into myself for the answers to questions like these that stir my soul.

~ Mary Kay Krause

Photo by Sheila Dierks

SEASONING THE SOUL

from "What Time is It?"

What time is it?
A simple question;
    a not-so-easy answer.

Time:
    we keep it;
    we manage it;
    we save it;
    we measure it;
    we waste it;
    we lose it.

Chronological time –
    the measure of marking when we work,
        when we play,
        when we pray,
        when we sleep,
        and when we rest.
Chronos—the span of linear time;
    a tool to measure the order of our lives.

Enter God's time—*Kairos*—

>a decisive point in time;
>where time becomes timeless;
>where life slows down;
>moments when we pray,
>>time seems endless;
>
>time enters a quiet solitude;
>time becomes gratitude
>>an amazing act of beauty.

A decisive point in time –
God's in-breaking moments into our lives.
God's time—the present moment.

~ Denise Pyles

SEASONING THE SOUL

Dwelling in Winter

Photo by Barbie Hull Photography

A Morning Intention

Each day I intend to be

stillness of dawn
presence of morn
fullness of midday
steadiness of afternoon
softness of eventide.

Intended to be Your bidding
with ease of night into day.

~ *Sharon Taylor*

I n pre-industrial times, when most people's lives were spent closely connected to nature's cycles, Samhain marked the moment for people to round up animals into the barns to protect them during the harsh months ahead. The last of the crops were put up for winter sustenance. People prepared for times of shared feasting and storytelling and the giving of thanks for the harvest.

Home fires would be lit from the central fire of the clan chief, and the time of darkness would be received. Lighting home fires from the central one reflected how much members of the community needed one another. Winter was—even as it is today—a precarious season. Many did not survive it. Then as now a caring community was needed to assure mutual survival when cold and dark deepened.

~ *Eileen Knoff*

Photo by Barbie Hull Photography

Thank you for the produce of our lives
and for the wonder of growth and accomplishment.

May we humbly know our need now to listen
and be still as we wait in darkness
for your word to take hold in each of us.

May this be a time of rich receptivity and a deepening
awareness of how You are within us and all around us:
in our breath, in our energy, in our joy.

~ Kathy McCarthy

A December Prayer

The lengthening of nighttime hours invites us
    to move inward, to embrace stillness,
Grant us the grace to enter the Great Mystery,
    that we may move beyond fear into peace,
that we may fully surrender in order
    to utter a wholehearted yes to you, O God.

Give us an open heart that we may experience
    the Oneness of all creation
    rather than to remain the observer.
For in the Oneness, we recognize the inner stirring
    of the Christ Child carried in humanity's womb.
And, in our encounter with all others,
    like Mary to Elizabeth,
    may we too discover stirrings of new life.

~ Sharon Taylor

Photo by Eileen Knoff

Rebirth

Star-kindling God
Shine into our depths,
Let us hear your voice within,
yearning,
calling,
pleading,
"Bring me to birth once again!"

Light bearing light,
Shine in our heart and soul,
Show us your fire again,
yearning,
calling,
pleading,
"Bring me to birth once again."

Amen.

~ William ("Rusty") Clyma

Uncovering the Light Within

Today, in the 21st century, humans have come to realize that perhaps the most important connection we need to make is with our own interiority, where Divine Light seeks to be received and embraced as being at the heart of our own complex psyche. Diverse faith expressions tell us that the human person carries an element of Divine Light within, a life that goes by many names.

It is our work to tend to that light, and to keep it lit, even when dark energies within and around us might seek to extinguish its flame. I have heard tell that a circle of Quakers coming together to discern the meaning of evil decided its essence was anything that sought to put out that Inner Light.

Perhaps so.

It is the gift of this winter season to hold open for us a time of emptiness, a womb-like space, inviting us to go deeper toward the place of our Inner Light. It can be the gift of dark moments that they lead us to an unexpected light within. I was graced with encountering such a light in the silent and dark moment of my own father's passing. That moment gave birth in me to new trust in the light at the heart of darkness.

As we allow ourselves to be more at home with that light within, we may discover within new thoughts about ourselves here on this earth—our value, our meaning, our purpose. We may begin to hear an inner sense assuring us of our inestimable value as an individual and as part of the human species.

Trusting we are of great value can encourage us to discover just what an inimitable reflection of Divine Life and Love we really are. Then we can allow that light to shine from the heart of our being through gifts we have been given to bring hope and love into the world.

I offer a simple prayer in ending this reflection:

May we be unafraid to walk through the darkness to the light within.
May we may find friends willing to walk with us who trust our inner light.
May the prayers, blessings, and reflections throughout these pages
and the spirituality of the Celtic-Christian world they reflect
be beacons guiding us toward safe harbor.

~ Eileen Knoff

Photo by Eileen Knoff

Releasing Winter

Samhain Blessing and Release

When the darkness comes,
may it be your dark loamy earth-time.
May your visions, like sleeping seeds,
be nourished by the dark.
May you be guided into wholly silence,
wholeness

~ *Victoria Rue*

Photo by Barbie Hull Photography

Closing Blessing

In the dark time of my father's death,
a light flashed forth,

piercing my back, driving through my heart,
and flowing forward into the emptiness.

May it be ever so,
that in our darkest days
Light will invade,

reassuring us we are not alone,

We are on the Way.

~ Eileen Knoff

Photo by Eileen Knoff

SEASONING THE SOUL

A Blessing for the New Year

O Holy Three-in-One,
as we begin another year of life
bless our senses with heightened awareness
to your Being, here and now.

Focus our sight through barren trees
to see horizons hidden in times of fullness.

Tune our hearing to the key of your love
that sings out to us in the whistling wind.

Tantalize us around the table of fellowship
with the smell of winter's broths and stews,
the taste of grains crafted into breads and brews,
the feel of a friend's understanding touch—
and silence.

~ *Eileen Knoff*

Photo by Barbie Hull Photography

Photo by Barbie Hull Photography

January Reflection

To trust in transformation
is January's work.

To be still as ice-laden trees
stand watch over the unseen decomposition
below the surface of things;

To know dis-integration as the only way
to recycle ourselves through the death-to-life pattern
that we must live: year-in, year-out—life-in, life-out.

Beneath our feet dead branches, petals, leaves and seeds
co-mingle with melting snows and bent light.
Chemicals conspire beneath the hard, brown crust.

No need to fear. We have crossed the threshold.

~ Eileen Knoff

SEASONING THE SOUL

Photo by Sheila Dierks

Breathe into your life ~

        Breathe into your death ~

Breathe into your life ~

        Breathe into your death ~

                Breathe into the whole

            ~ Victoria Rue

Two Haikus

Snow falls at midnight.
Grey fox moves without a sound.
God speaks in silence

Winter and Springtime,
Each other's *Anam Cara*
God Speaks in silence

~ David Garner

SEASONING THE SOUL

Questions for Reflection by Individuals or Groups

Before entering into reflection on the questions in each section, it may be helpful to take a moment to look over the section again, recalling what most affected you when you first perused the material, and what seems to speak to you most now.

In the *America* magazine of October 27, 2008 spiritual writer Margaret Silf wrote: "Often all God needs to bring new insights to birth are empty space and unrushed time." What arises in you as you read this comment? How do you feel about what arises in you?

Which if any of the writings or photographs in this Samhain (Winter) section seemed to help you open up to empty space and unrushed time, even if only briefly?

Explore this further. What was it about those items that helped you?

Was there anything in your encounter with these words or pictures that disturbed you?

Questions for Reflection

What might that be about for you?

Several different questions were scattered throughout this section. Did any of them cause you to pause and become aware of something you hadn't realized before? What did you realize?

What has been starting to take root in the darkness of these past several months for you?

Consider undertaking a form of art to contemplate this more, such as writing, drawing, music, gardening, quilting, glasswork, beadwork, dance, creation of ritual, or whatever other art form you enjoy, and notice what this artwork calls forth out of you.

Welcome, Brigit,

Welcome over our threshold.
We welcome the wisdom and gifts that you bring for our use.

By offering blessing and grace to our daily lives,
help us manifest what our winter dreams have beckoned us to create.
Nourish the green shoots of our new lives.

~ *Jane Comerford*

Photo by Liz Knoff Floodeen

SEASONING THE SOUL

Photo by Barbie Hull Photography

Imbolc, Candelmas
The lactation of the ewes
Winter births the spring

~ from David Garner's *Imbolc*

The Season of Imbolc (Spring)

Do you hear it clearly?
That what you are enveloped in is the body of God
what you were born from is the mother of Life.

~ Jan Phillips, from *No Ordinary Time*

SEASONING THE SOUL

Entering Spring

Our Celtic Brigit was goddess of poetry, song and wisdom.
So now in the dead and dark of winter, let us
gather around the flame that is her legacy.

> Let us sing out winter songs and read aloud our rhymes
> And gain from them the wisdom that comes in darkest times.
> For it is the sacred feminine from cold will Brigit bring.
> And then at last, like ages past,
> She will midwife the spring.

>> St. Brigit, fire of Kildare,
>> Goddess of the hearth
>> Warm us till the spring.
>>
>> ~ from David Garner's *Imbolc*

Photo by Eileen Knoff

About Imbolc

The Celtic people, so closely tied to the land for survival, took their cues for seasonal change from the agricultural cycle. Thus, February 1 marks the beginning of spring on the Celtic Calendar, a season once called Imbolc. The word refers to the time when ewes come into milk to feed their newborn lambs and new life begins to emerge from the soil.

Come Imbolc, the gently lengthening light tugs at what lies hidden beneath the earth, giving crocus tips and daffodil stems courage to push up through the still hard ground. With those signs of life, internal fears of the deadliness of winter (especially in times before central heating) could subside. Hearing again the songs of returning birds who had taken refuge in warmer climes, people could begin to breathe a bit easier and hope that winter's worst was behind them.

Given the returning signs of life in spring, it comes as no surprise that pre-Christian Celts associated this time of year with one of their primary female gods, Brigit (variously spelled Brigid, Bridgid, Bridget, and Bride). Mythology linked Brigid to midwifery, ironworking, poetry, and the hearth. Once Christianity predominated in Ireland, the name Brigid came to refer to a sixth-century founder of a monastery in Kildare, Ireland. One of Patrick's most renowned converts, over time this Brigid of Kildare has come to stand as patroness of Ireland. Purportedly the daughter of a druid priest and his Christian slave woman, Brigid serves as an example and symbol for how practices of the earlier druidic religious perspective were blended in many ways with later Christian ones.

Legends abound of this saint's compassion as the abbess of a Christian monastery and as a bishop, or overseer. One of the legends about Brigid alluded to later in this section is that of her cloak. In this fantastic fable, Brigid asks a chieftain for land for her monastery. He is reluctant to share, so he offers a deal he believes will favor him. Brigid can have whatever land her mantle, or cloak, can cover. When she lays her mantle on the ground, it expands to cover the land as far as the eye can see. The king learns to share and we who hear the story learn of the abundance that comes to the one who lives in trust and generosity.

Jane Comerford, spiritual director at the Osage Forest of Peace, has called Brigid "an image for the creative powers that foster newness in our lives." (*Brigid's Circle*, Februrary 2011).

~ Eileen Knoff

Mothering God,

like Brigid at Her forge,
purge the dross
from my heart and spirit.
Make me pliable, yet strong,
forming me with Your Skillful Love.

Mothering God,
like Brigid at Her hearth,
kindle all that is bright and warm in me
for the sake of my children,
my friends, my neighbors,
all lives I may touch,
and for the sake of my soul.

Mothering God,
like Brigid at the end of the day,
smoor the embers of my unbelief
and sweep away all despair,
unrest, and confusion,
that I may trust
in Your kindness always,
ashes to ashes, dust to dust.

So may it be.

~ Cheryl Anne

An Opening Blessing

May these initial days of Imbolc, Celtic Spring,
    usher in the spirit that whispers new life,

May our hearts be warmed by hope-filled stirrings
    as we emerge from winter's darkness,

And, may we recognize and be grateful for insights
    that took form in the fallow days of winter.

May we nurture seeds of hope, love and longed-for peace,
    planted at a time when these virtues seemed all too distant.

And, just as the seedling breaks free from the shell
    that served as its protective barrier,
May we, too, recognize those aspects of our lives
    that no longer serve and trust the process of letting go.

For truly, as the seedling is called forth
    from the tomb that once protected it,
So too, are we called to become as the One imagined.

                  ~ Sharon Taylor

Photo by Barbie Hull Photography

Dwelling in Spring

May the promise of lengthening Light
lift burdens lying behind you now
to reveal a gift in wounds
you have suffered.

May you rise up in compassion, in grace
in the trust of Love that lies within,
Love that lifts you out of shadows
into the embrace that burns and bathes.

~ Eileen Knoff

Photo by Barbie Hull Photography

Dwelling in Spring

Photo by Kris Jenkins

May Brigid bless the house wherein you dwell
bless every fireside, every wall and door,
bless every heart that beats beneath its roof,
bless every hand that toils to bring it joy,
bless every foot that walks its portals through,
May Brigid bless the house that shelters you.

~ Traditional Celtic blessing

The Soul's Soft Shelter

Of the many houses that shelter us, there are two I want to ask Brigid to bless as we move into the Celtic month of Imbolc: the Earth itself, for generously providing us with all we need to live, and our souls, which the Celts believed surrounded the body, and served as the body's true shelter.

I realize that I risk looking superstitious by asking Brigid to bless anything in our practical age. Isn't she long dead, if she ever really lived? Aren't the superhuman stories told about her more fantasy than reality? A materialistic or analytic mind might say so and urge me to let her image go. I am, however, more a literary and contemplative type. I take a different view. I find in Brigid an icon that lasts because it can shelter some of the values many of us hold most dear today—values like justice and mercy, compassion and generosity. These values pervade the legends celebrating Brigid's life and give her legends their staying power.

Whether a woman named Brigid lived exactly as the stories tell us she did—turning water into beer, conjuring up lost items for people, or restoring missing limbs—is not what matters to me. In Brigid's story we have a symbol that can help us co-create the just and generous earth community we long for—a community led wisely by women and men together in a spirit of graciousness and compassion rather than in violent competition.

When I ask Brigid to bless the earth and bless our souls, I am really naming my deep desire that humanity remain faithful to our best selves. I am hoping we will not waver in our determination to walk into places of oppression and carry out justice, to seek to heal where we find disease, or to educate where opportunities are few. When I ask Brigid to bless, I am asking that we will remain true to our soul's soft shelter, where Divine Light refuses to let powers of darkness have the final word.

~ Eileen Knoff

Under the Cloak of Brigid

Brigid comes with the confidence of the oak tree
to those with a waiting heart.

She comes to people who are eager to touch
the fabric of her wisdom cloak.

Celtic Brigid, wide is your cloak of wisdom!

Gift us with expansive minds and hearts,
weave wisdom and hospitality into the marrow of our bones.

Brigid, wrap your cloak around us,
our wounded souls anoint.

Enable us to delight in the cream of our own goodness.
May we hold a space in our hearts for each other's beauty.

Brigid of Ireland, cradle us, drape your cloak
about us and gaze upon us with love in the coming year.

May the gift of wisdom be our gift to each other
as we celebrate you with joy!

~ Sr. Anna Hennessy, C.S.B.

SEASONING THE SOUL

The Giveaway

Pulitzer Prize winner Phyllis McGinley composed a warm and whimsical poem about Saint Brigid entitled, "The Giveaway," in which she describes Brigid's propensity for the reckless, radical giving away of all manner of food and possessions, much to the chagrin of her father. The poem has its basis in various legends surrounding the life of the saint. Although there are many aspects of Brigid's character to which I relate and aspire, it is her natural generosity which I find most endearing. Perhaps it's that I understand that impulse to bless.

As a child I was guilty of "Robin Hood Syndrome," stealing from my atheist father's wallet to fill the alms box at the church affiliated with my school. Little did I realize that we were not really "rich" by most standards. It seemed to me we had plenty and could certainly stand to share. I also gave away my toys, books, record albums; anything I thought someone else might enjoy. I gave away clothing and food to a little girl down the street who seemed to be in need. I never bothered to ask permission. So, stumbling upon such stories of Brigid caused me instantly to take her as a kinswoman and friend.

With my Beloved Brigid I have discovered that great Joy of the Giveaway: of possessions, of time, of heart. As I write this, I am reminded of the Native American concept of "Giveaway," which I first encountered while on retreat with the Benedictine Sisters of Erie, Pennsylvania many years ago, in which an object retains its blessedness only as long and as far as it stays in motion—being given, and given, and given again.

And I have found that the most valuable gift any of us has to offer is that of quiet, respectful presence with another. This we can indeed give away again and again and again, with opportunities for presence arising most every day. It is such simple loving kindness that warms the heart, like the first breath of spring. Love, the sweet sap and lifeblood of all existence.

~ Cheryl Anne

Mystery of Growing Light and Waning Dark,
You surprise this changing world.

Each season bears its own gift,
O Mother of the longer day, yours
is an invitation to us
into your gift of sun-tide, both in the morning as
we rise, and in the evening as we dine.

Let us honor the life force reawakening
as all that has died to bring freshness claims its place.
Let us kiss the earth of all renewed creation.

~ *Sheila Dierks*

Photo by Liz Knoff Floodeen

SEASONING THE SOUL

I stand, stand on the knife-sharp edge of equinox
Steady now . . .
Maintain balance.
Now gently look behind . . .
Have the dark months graced me?

Photo by Eileen Knoff

. . . Now, steady still, I turn toward the light.
What do I see?
What glows?

. . . All life is treasure: what lies behind
And what cannot yet be known.
So, balance . . . balance . . .
Bless equilibrium.

~ excerpts from a reflection by Sheila Dierks

From March Musings

More and more I believe that I am called to trust the value in both what delights and what disturbs. Together they become the food for our growth. I see this truth as I observe the seasonal cycle. Every year dead leaves and branches feed the seeds while winter rains speed along decomposition. That which seems dark and dismal sustains us in transformation's womb, until green shoots once again stretch for the sky.

Death of what has been, year in and year out, is the source that enables everything to come into its own. Why then does it feel so hard to accept death's presence and value it as vital to the emergence of new life?

According to Celtic philosopher John O'Donohue, struggling with the energy of opposites within ourselves begins "an integrity of transfiguration and not the mere replacement of image, surface, or one system by another."

Remaining faithful to engaging the contradictory energies that lie within can, Donohue assures, lead us to a harmony deeper than any contradiction. He reminds us to be patient with this process, assuring us that if we do, a new courage will take shape that empowers us to engage life's "depth, danger, and darkness." (*Anam Cara*, pp. 114-15.)

~ *Eileen Knoff*

Photo by Eileen Knoff

SEASONING THE SOUL

May you find new life bursting forth out of deep shadow.
May who you are and what you are meant to be gain clarity of shape and direction.
May you live ever more into that for which your heart most hopes.

~ Eileen Knoff

Photo by Barbie Hull Photography

April Blessing

May we spring at spring's awakening
    like the bulbs hiding in the earth
May we awaken, stretch and become
    the secret selves that God alone sees
    may we awaken and become.

May we break free and grow
    like chicks newly hatched
May we cease to be enclosed in hardened shells
    And reveal what God has always loved
    may we cease to be enclosed.

May we look upon each other
    seeing beyond what first appears
May we know that each is created by love
    created lovable and desirable beyond our knowing
    may we look upon each other.

May the seeing of each other bring a blessing
    like warm rains bring spring bulbs to life
May the seeing of each other be a brooding warmth
    encouraging the transformation of hardened hearts
    may the seeing of each other be with love.

~ Kedda Keough

SEASONING THE SOUL

Photo by Eileen Knoff

To Brigid

Holy Brigid, Bride, you lead me home today,
Queen of Love, showing me my own true heart,
Fire ever lit, flowing milk that does not cease
to fill the hungry poor and give captives sure release,
your compassion calls me out: *Here is your part:*
to gather, listen, share, forgive and pray.

These seem so little, merely straw and coal
to stave off winter's howling winds
and certain death. Yet, still, I know
myself as called to take the plunge below
and enter Your Well of Wisdom, facing sins
of generations past: *Woman, be made whole!*

~ Eileen Knoff

Releasing Spring

Contemplating Creation

Whether waiting for bulbs to break ground, entering into new relationships or following new dreams, we are being invited during this season into new life, which draws us toward love, the divine flow of creativity.

~ Mary Ellen Robertson

Creation is by no means finished. All we have to do is look at life around us and, aided by things like the Hubble telescope, space ships that travel to Jupiter or beyond, or electron microscopes that peer into the tiniest specs of the universe; we know that Creation continues and is unfolding.

~ Kedda Keough

As the snows melt and my flower garden begins its stirring, I wonder if the spring bulbs imagine the blossoms they will become as they let go of their shrouds and break through the crusty soil. They became as divinely planned. What then of my becoming?

~ Sharon Taylor

Releasing Spring

Photo by Eileen Knoff

Letting go to live our dreams

A release of spring calls us to action that supports the development of life in ourselves and around ourselves. The time feels ripe to let go of thoughts of scarcity that the dark months may have stirred up in us. Abundance awaits us as summer beckons us onward.

This abundance lies not only around us on and in the land, but within us, for we too are of the earth. We have been called "earth come to consciousness," by paleontologist/priest Pierre Teilhard de Chardin. We are filled with an abundance of desires, longings, dreams, visions. And this inner life is meant to come to an outer manifestation. The emergence is over and now we put our hands to the plowshares. We turn our attention to care and nurture of this new life so that it can reach its fulfillment.

What we dream, we can bring to life. We must just take a first step, through the open gate and into the field beyond.

And then, we take a second step further into the open, trusting more and more in what we deeply desire. For some this means dreams of justice—gathering in a harvest of food for the hungry, or bringing together a planetary community of mutual respect in the midst of our differences. For we are here, on spaceship Earth, sharing a common planet, and a common past as well as a common future.

Many of us have heard of the quotation often attributed to Goethe. I believe it bears repeating as we move through spring toward summer:

> Whatever you can do or dream, begin it
> Boldness has genius, power, and magic in it.

~ Eileen Knoff

SEASONING THE SOUL

May the Precious and Powerful Divine Presence
touch us with a permeating, freeing Love,
inspiring us to release all we do not truly need
and to embrace the Sacred Security of Spirit
in Whom there is no lack.
May the storehouse of our hearts
be filled to bursting as we join in the Great Giveaway
with Blessed Brigid of Ireland and all those who walk in Love's Lavish Way.

Amen. And so it is.

~ Cheryl Anne

To cross the threshold from emergence to fulfillment,
to trust water cutting underfoot
where no eye can reach,
to believe in how the story ends
with acorn rising to great oak
and Great Oak giving gracious shade long after
my life has faded from fullness.

~ Eileen Knoff

Photo by Eileen Knoff

On the Well's Edge

The late spring day I met my first Irish well
I tiptoed gingerly on the rocky green land
as if through quicksand.

I feared slipping into the black
Aran Isle soil,
sliding like Alice down the tunnel,
kicking about, neck-high in black water
lost in a crazy world not of my making—
or maybe indeed of my creating—
flailing about foolishly.

I did not tumble in;
instead I paced and chanted
'round the well's edge,
circling the circumference with fellow pilgrims.

Photo by Eileen Knoff

Afterward, we hiked to a nearby standing stone and crumbling altar
which in turn led to an ancient archway;
through its opening I beheld
tall grasses and the sea beyond,
where heaven's horizon loomed.

~ *Eileen Knoff*

SEASONING THE SOUL

Questions for Reflection by Individuals or Groups

What is coming to life in you or around you this season of Spring? How do you want to respond to that emergence of new life?

What meaning do you make of the phrase: "Winter births the spring?"

What aspects of Brigid do you find most striking? Does that reveal anything new to you about yourself?

What of this section's reflections or images most delight you, surprise you, challenge you, console you?

Questions for Reflection

What do you find yourself most desiring to nurture and protect in this Spring season?

Are there changes you want to make to be able to fully enter the springtime of your life right now?

Brigid's priestesses and later the nuns at Kildare kept her fire burning. What is the fire burning in you, and what helps you keep that fire burning?

Is there anything you need or want to release so that the new within you can take root and blossom?

If you were to choose an artistic form to depict what is emerging in your life what form would it take? Consider creating this form.

SEASONING THE SOUL

Photo by Liz Knoff Floodeen

A Beltane Blessing

May the blessing of light be on you—
Light without and light within.
May the blessed sunlight shine on you
And warm your heart
till it glows like a great peat fire.

~ traditional—often called "Old Celtic Blessing"

The Season of Beltane (Summer)

Delightful is the season's splendor,
rough winter has gone,
white is every fruitful wood,
a joyous peace in summer.

~ from *The Boyhood Deeds of Fionn MacCumhail*

SEASONING THE SOUL

Entering Summer

Photo by Eileen Knoff

Always Present and Ever Living One,

Our hearts are filled with gratitude for this time when life flows back into the earth after a long winter. May this be our time for extinguishing the old and lighting new fires of purification. May our hearts be renewed to partake in the passion of loving relationships and a commitment to serve all creation. Come and let us emblazon the world together!

~ Scott Jenkins

Entering Summer

About Beltane

Centuries ago, on the evening before the daybreak of Beltane, a singular fire was lit high upon the hill. The Druid blessed and prayed, while all who gathered sang and gave thanks. The ranks closed around this *one* fire. Everyone stared at the *one* flame, as the medieval philosopher Eriugena would say centuries later, "which would ignite the world with a passion for God!"

The silence was broken abruptly by the Druid's commission, "Go! Go, now!" The runners would thrust their torches into the fire; departing in silence they would go. *It was time!* It was the time to pass the flame, to signal a light in the darkness, to bring hopeful shadows to their loved ones.

The horseriders were the next to plunge their torches into the flames. The galloping hooves thundered upon the road, the riders filled with holy fervor to carry this sacred heat.

Photo by Diane Ahern Photography

Beltane's gift, its mission within, is to rekindle this holy, life-embracing passion. Can you feel its energy? Are you sensing the thinness of the veil between this world and the next? Where is the life-giving fire longing to be re-lit within your life?

Often our religion seeks to keep life on an even keel. It is a subtle move for reasons long since forgotten and every day believed. There is a fear around our passions, one which we can all understand.

The call is both *from* and *to* fire. Listen. Let us remember a deeper truth than the fear of an institution or the trepidation found on the surface of our hearts. Our passion is the fire within to transform, purify, and enjoy the world!

~ Scott Jenkins

Beltane Blossoms

Beltane week bursts upon us,
in brilliant color
announcing Summer's opening dance.

Blooming petals unfold in the gracious sun,
longed-for gift after a cold, dark winter.
Spring's breakthrough work behind,
stems and leaves sway now in warmer breezes.

We too step lightly out of doors
more often than we did before,
soaking in generous warmth,

Oh wondrous time of simple presence
and gentle reception!

Beltane bloom, teach us now
and everyday, to lift face and hands
toward our Gentle Gardener's
gracious love, tender of us all.

Together, let us grow in gratitude,
reaching upward toward the light
and bowing downward
to what burns in our secret depths.

~ Eileen Knoff

Entering Summer

Photo by Barbie Hull Photography

A Summer Prayer

As we enter this season of resurgence
May the warming rays of the sun
Bring forth in our hearts
Blossoms of love for all.

May the land upon which we rely
Prosper and provide nourishment
Even as we nourish one another
With the spirit of loving grace.

~ Roger McClellan

SEASONING THE SOUL

Holy One of Infinite Love,
your fragrance of grace wafts upon us
like the scent of fresh rain upon blooming earth.
As new life buds forth from the sacred soil,
nudge us to lean into the dark
with a waking heart and keen awareness
to your Spirit breaking forth like the morning dawn—
re-creating us anew in love once more.
May your blessing grow our hope
in the dawning of a new day,
a new season, a new moment.

~ Denise Pyles

Photo by Eileen Knoff

One Perfect Moment

The perfect moment took me by surprise that Saturday in early June.

The sun was nearing high noon as I stood in a memorial rose garden on the green at George Fox College, south of Portland. I had never been to this spot before, and was only here now because I had been invited to attend an ordination ceremony set to start in less than an hour just down the road. Having been asked to participate in an opening procession, my husband and I planned ahead so as to be sure to be on time. As it turned out, we were early enough to stop our car at the college green to stretch our legs before heading indoors for the service.

It was a rare treat for me to be in Oregon in June out among the roses on a sunny day. I love roses, and in June the roses in Oregon are so lovely that the city celebrates with a festival, which happened to be occurring that very day in downtown Portland. Being in the region was enough; I didn't miss the crowds of the festival. I liked the simplicity of the college green late on Saturday morning, a few students lying on the grass under towering evergreens that stretched into a clear blue sky. My husband, who had accompanied me, stood under the trees as well, waiting.

I studied the labels of the roses, finding a few favorites—the deep red Abraham Lincoln and the creamy Peace. Pausing to look down, I saw beside me a rich yellow-orange rose tinged in red staring up at me. Captivated, I sought out her name: Perfect Moment. How apropos! All of a sudden I realized the name was not only of the rose, but this place, and time, and my being here. Opening to the moment, I heard a campus carillon begin to strike noon. Bells blended with roses, my joy deepened and time itself stood still. Then, on the final stroke of twelve, a lone bird sang out, awakening me to my life.

~ Eileen Knoff

Dwelling in Summer

A Summer Blessing

May we be open in this season of flowering
to show forth beauty.

for soon will come the pruning sheers,
and the cutback.

Then, again we will need to wait,
for our flowering.

May we be willing now
to become flower.

May we be today
the Beauty that we are,

waiting, ever waiting,
even as we bloom.

~ *Eileen Knoff*

Photo by Liz Knoff Floodeen

A bit more about Beltane

For the early Celts Beltane brought celebrations of the sun's return, and with it the return of fertility. Cattle were released from winter quarters and driven between fires that were believed to have cleansing properties. Animals were mated; humans enjoyed feasts and fairs and games. Beltane was also a time when trial marriages could be dissolved and new relationships begun to be explored.

Beltane specifically referred to the name of the Gaulish god Belenos, the Shining One. The name is not unlike the one Christians often give to Jesus, as the Christ, the Light of the World. Seeing Christ as the Light of the world would not have been a strange idea to the Celts, for even before the Christian gospel was spread around the British Isles, there was a God of Light, and this was the season of that god.

As in the Christian story, light and love were intertwined to bring life to humans, and to all creation. Lighting bonfires and decking holy wells were also common practices with the arrival of Beltane (Bealtaine, pronounced BYELL-ten-uh, in Irish) and by midsummer, the gift of light would be celebrated by leaping over the ashes of bonfires.

A Litha (Midsummer) Reflection

Litha, longest day
And night of the Faerie Folk;
All bless St. John's Eve.

This halfway point between Beltane and Lughasadh is a time of power and passion. The sun is at its apex and crops are full and promise a bountiful harvest. It is a sensuous time when darkness is held at bay. We now celebrate our five senses and know that our God is a god of passion as well as purpose. We are alive and life is to be lived to its fullest.

Aine, fairy queen,
Midsummer Anam Cara;
Let us leap the fire.

~ David Garner

SEASONING THE SOUL

Photo by Eileen Knoff

O Source of the Summer Sun,
You call us forth this time of year
into our fullest blooming.

Lure us into Your Loving Life.
Let our blooms entice the blooming of all around us
into their own full flowering.

May our gentle presence, simple listening, and outstretched hands
be a path through Your Garden,
a Way into the Beauty that lies within everyone, everything.

~ Eileen Knoff

Blessing of the Five Senses

May you walk this day
with a mindfulness of God
all around you and within.
For God is beneath the ground of your feet.
God is within the grasp of your touch.
The fragrance of God lingers in the air under your nose.
The sound of God pulsates in your ear's drum.
God's taste of love is placed upon your lips.
God is within your vision
This moment, this day, every day of your life.
May you walk this day with a mindfulness of God. Amen.

~ Denise Pyles in *A Glowing Ember of Courage*

SEASONING THE SOUL

Brendan and Beltane: the Saint of the Season

I share my birthday with the feast day of St. Brendan the Voyager. Brendan is a member of what has become known as the Second Order of Irish Saints. This group is credited with preserving numerous great works of civilization during the Dark Ages, when many of Europe's cultural artifacts and books were destroyed following the collapse of the Roman Empire.

According to legend, Brendan and a number of fellow monks traveled widely, including the legendary journey in search of the mythical Land of Promise. Without benefit of any navigational coordinates, Brendan and his crew set out, trusting that God would guide them in their journey.

It seems to me that these stories of the blessed Brendan are very analogous to our own existence as we witness the birth of new communities with simultaneously fresh and age-old expressions of faith. While we may, like Brendan, have no knowledge of the coordinates of our destination, may we travel together boldly, and trusting in the Spirit as She calls us ever onward.

> Our Great and wonderful Father God,
> hearken us near to your voice.
> Blessed Mother Spirit,
> hold us in your loving embrace,
> that so emboldened by your strength and nurture
> we might, like Blessed Brendan
> navigate those waters of uncertainty
> as we seek the blessings that you hold.
> May we find in you and each other,
> companions along the journey
> and the safe embrace of harbor.
>
> *~ Roger McClellan*

Photo by Eileen Knoff

On Fire

Dare I trust the fire
within
flashing forth,

A tiny spark

encircled by a compassion that becomes passion
for justice, mercy, love,
freedom,
peace,
joy

The passion of the ruby red rose
Whose aroma permeates the garden.
It is that kind of fire that insists on burning
No rains can dampen the flames
though I might set myself out for days and days in the rain

the fire will not go out.

"I have come to set a Fire on the Earth
and how I wish it were burning already."

~ Eileen Knoff

Dwelling in Summer

Photo by Liz Knoff Floodeen

SEASONING THE SOUL

Photo by Barbie Hull Photography

Reflection

I bask in the glow of the Light, that Light resonating like a symphony with its beginning, its middle, and its circle back into a spiral of connectedness, weaving its many strands together. In the beginning of this symphony, I care. I feel the pain but don't know what to do about it; I feel the oneness of all creation, the universe, but I am lost.

And as I slowly move into the next movement, notes of discord appear. Oh, I feel the pain, the crushing sense of injustice I see all around me. I feel the pain of distrust, the self-centered passions denying justice to those who suffer. I search for those notes of peace and compassion I know must be hiding behind the discord.

Trusting in the promise of "the glory you gave me," I create new notes, melding them with those hidden. I reach out and touch this light—I change myself, I appeal to the God-ness in all. My sense of oneness quiets the discord with notes of compassion, justice, healing, creating a changed flow, changed movement, one that builds to a towering crescendo of overwhelming love, healing the ruptures.

In the end, this symphony of light has a final movement where discord is gone, and the harmony of justice and compassion allows me to experience my connectedness in and with God. In the symphony of the light, we all are one.

~ Mandy Bennett

Releasing Summer

Photo by Barbie Hull Photography

O GOD, who brought me from the rest of last night
Unto the joyous light of this day,
Be Thou bringing me from the new light of this day
Unto the guiding light of eternity.
    Oh! from the new light of this day
    Unto the guiding light of eternity.

        ~ From the *Carmina Gadelica*, vol 1

Photo by Barbie Hull Photography

God of light,

Mother of love,

Father of peace,

Envelop us in the harmony of your symphony.
Allow justice and compassion to flow through us to others,

Honoring our connectedness with all.

Amen.

~ Mandy Bennett

Midsummer Reflection

Sometimes our spiritual journey can be like Western Washington weather—day after day of gray sameness; we wonder if we can endure it. We yearn for life to have meaning. We yearn for God's spirit to once again set our hearts on fire, and set us in motion. We pray: Come Holy Spirit, breathe us into life.

When our prayer is answered and the warmth of God's Spirit grows stronger within us, setting fire in our hearts, we once again burn with God's love. This, our spiritual summer, is a time of gratitude and rejoicing for the gifts of God, especially the gift of the Holy Spirit within us that gets us moving.

~ Kedda Keough

As Certain as the Sun

This spring has been an extraordinarily tumultuous time here in the southern United States. An unprecedented severity of storms with floods and deadly tornadoes has been an intense reminder of the frailty of human life. The residents of affected areas have rallied to help neighbors and to grieve with them as well. We have prayed, we have cried, and we have waited for summer. Thankfully, in the great springtime battle between the remnant of winter's dark and chill and summer's promise of light and warmth, summer is bound to win . . . eventually.

It is a comfort to recognize this same truth in the constantly changing seasons of our lives, as we face our times of darkness and when our hearts and hopes grow cold. We all at some point navigate the upheaval of great change and wonder if life will ever settle down, if we will indeed again welcome the warmth of peace and longed-for Reign of Light.

Thanks be to God for that precious Light born from the darkness and tumult, for the Peace after the storms, and for the Unfailing Love which invites, receives, and warms us always . . . as certain as the sun.

~ Cheryl Anne

Becoming

The lush rose blooms cause limbs to bow
with the weight of their beauty.
Through its profuse display
the rose bush holds nothing back.
It comes into its fullness freely, joyously,
bountifully.

Inspire us, O Divine Creator, to step fully into our becoming.
Renew us with the faith of little children.
Like these little ones, let us not question possibility.

~ Sharon Taylor

SEASONING THE SOUL

Photo by Kris Jenkins

Play

Most Gracious and Loving Creator,
teach us anew to play.
Call out our inner child whose laughter
bubbles up freely.

Bring forth the child within who finds joy in the passing butterfly,
in the rabbits nibbling at the edge of the garden each morning,
and in the parade of pelicans who dip and bob their heads below the pond's surface,
using their beaks to scoop up Your abundance.

Remind us that joy is found in more ways than we can count.
As the poet Rumi advised so many years ago,
teach us to sell our cleverness and to buy bewilderment.

~ Sharon Taylor

Closing Prayer

Beloved One,
Heaven's Bright Sun,
Bring us to Fullness of Light.

Guide us to stillness
By grace of your Brilliance
As we prepare once again for the night.

Amen.

~ *Cheryl Anne*

Photo by Barbie Hull Photography

SEASONING THE SOUL

Questions for Reflection by Individuals or Groups

What have you found in this section to delight you, surprise you, challenge you, or console you?

What is coming to fullness in your life these days?

How are you finding time to rest or play in the fullness of this season?

What have you discovered as you have spent time with these blessings, reflections, prayers and images about your relationship with Summer—and with your own soul?

Questions for Reflection

Which, if any, of the words, images, or ideas of the old Celtic ways most remain with you after you close this book and go about your day? What is that about for you?

Is there anything you might want to do differently in your life to fully embrace Summer's light and life?

Is there anything you need or want to release of this Summer experience so that you can make room for the harvest months still to comes?

As Summer ends, what remains? Consider creating something to image this remnant of Summer.

Opening Blessing

Good tidings,
Sea fruitful

Shellfish plentiful,
Woods smile,

Fruit-tress ripening,
Wheat fields grow,

Bee-swarms are many,
A radiant world;
Kindly summer,
Tidings good.

~ Irish, *The Colloquy of the Two Sages*, 10th century
~ contributed by Jane Comerford

Photo by Barbie Hull Photography

The Season of Lughnasadh (Autumn)

May all who read these words be blessed
and know the old ways are not dead
Lughnasadh now has come again;
So let us all our troubles shed.

~ David Garner

SEASONING THE SOUL

Entering Autumn

Photo by Anna Hennessy, C.S. B.

I sense a shift in the air before
    seeing evidence of change.
The knowing comes before the realization.
Silence one day,
    the ringing of locusts' song the next.
Perhaps they sing an invitation to make ready,
    to prepare for the time of harvest.
Looking upon the bounty,
    observing how grace transformed seeds
    planted by the Divine.
Humbled,
    I bow in thanksgiving.

~ *Sharon Taylor*

August Reflection

Lughnasadh (pronounced Loo-nah-sah), traditionally celebrated on August 1, stands as the mid-point between the Summer Solstice and the Autumnal Equinox. Lughnasadh takes its name from one of the chief god figures of the Celtic mythology, Lugh. It is said that Lugh dedicated this festival to his mother, Tailtu, whose name means, "The Great One of the Earth." Tailtu might be taken then as a personification of the Earth itself.

This threshold time invites us to let go of our concerns about the coming winter and the missed opportunities of the past spring. The very colors that surround us invite us to live in the moment, to acknowledge the fecundity of the earth beneath our feet.

If we are willing to embrace this most sensuous time of the year, we can begin to understand what the Celtic tradition has long known: humans have two sources from which to draw our knowledge of God: the Holy Texts of the various faith traditions, and Nature. In nature all of the lessons of Christ's teachings are evident. To discover this we simply need to be present to the moment.

May the following prayer serve to move us into this new season as we listen to our Celtic heritage:

Photo by Diane Ahern Photography

SEASONING THE SOUL

Photo by Kris Jenkins

Mother-Father God,
We ask the following questions
knowing full well that you have
already provided the answers:

When Sister Maple Leaf pirouettes down
Resplendent in her crimson gown
And then lies prostrate on the ground,
Is not that Christ's Reflection?

And when Brother Aspen, tall and bold,
In autumn sheds his cloak of gold
Then in the Spring green leaves unfold
Is not that resurrection?

You see, all of the tales that the scriptures tell
Are told in nature just as well.
Here on earth are both heaven and hell.
It's a story told over and over.

So Mother-Father here is our plea:
May you bless Brigid's family
And help us each find the Trinity
In every leaf of clover.

~ David Garner

A Harvest Reflection

August arrives with the celebration of Lughnasadh; fruits of the earth begin to blanket our tables. Many of us find ourselves blessed beyond measure with the abundance of a good harvest.

I recall today the beauty and the bounty of our family's vegetable garden, which I took for granted in my youth. It was so easy then to go out and pick ripe squash, green beans and ears of corn. We spent hours canning and freezing to make sure we had enough food for the winter to come.

Now, more conscious of another kind of harvest in my life, I find myself gathering my thoughts: *What are the interior fruits that I am harvesting from past plantings? What gifts of the Spirit has the "wild goose" brought into my life this past summer? What must I start now to release to be open to the new still ahead of me?*

~ Jane Comerford

Photo by Barbie Hull Photography

SEASONING THE SOUL

Photo by Eileen Knoff

Autumn Mantra

Autumn God,

Enable us to embrace the events that fall onto our path.

Help us to consecrate them on the table of daily living.

On our pilgrim journey, may we welcome each

interruption that life offers us and allow it to become part

of our Autumn mantra.

~ Anna Hennessy, C.S.B.

Berry Picking

Summer fullness has come to fruit at last
in the shape of berries, black and lush upon the vine
easy to the touch, falling to the earth as food
for now, and for next year's growth as well.

The children led me there.
I found them suddenly, while on a walk some weeks ago.
eager to test the taste well before full grown
they burst forth purple and laughing, from the bushes.

"Are the berries ready?" I queried.
"Not yet," they replied,
"still a little sour." Their faces puckered.

Photo by Liz Knoff Floodeen

Soon then, I remember saying,
recalling now their joyful spirits
and kindness to a stranger,
hard to find in these trying times,
those sorts of times the sages say will try men's souls.
And women's too, perhaps even more than the men's.

The fruit is ready now, ripe upon the vine,
falling into my bowl, barely an effort for me
or the berries. Some are even more ready
and fall straight to earth to die.

I will retrieve enough for my ritual cobbler
near Labor Day, my end-of-summer celebration.
I take enough, and leave the rest for guests who follow,
to pick and to enjoy the way *they* most desire.

I move along toward home, grateful, always grateful,
for earth that dies each year, so we may live,
inviting a like response, so hard to give.

~ Eileen Knoff

SEASONING THE SOUL

Dwelling in Autumn

. . . in approach of the equinox

We stand now in the balance of day and night.
May the blessing of new life discovered in Christ
make us fearless each time we are called
more deeply into days of darkness.
May we always trust the light to return.

May we learn to let go
so we may be ready to embrace
what comes new into our lives.

~ Kedda Keough

Photo by Kris Jenkins

The Way of the Labyrinth

September is the time of endings: the last summer picnic, a last day at the beach, a final hike in the woods. It is also the time of beginnings: a new school year, a renewed focus on our work, and the arrival of the autumnal equinox, which tips the balance of light ever so slightly toward the darkness.

Soon I will facilitate some participants of *Brigid's Circle* and friends in the greater Puget Sound region in a worship on the labyrinth at Edmonds Christian Church. I have led labyrinth walks there many times, both indoors and outdoors, traveling its paths in all kinds of weather and in every season.

Photo by Eileen Knoff

For me, the most poignant moments with the labyrinth come in early fall as I inhale the aroma of the lingering summer blooms. In these times I hear a faint sighing, like the very voice of winter, whispering, "I am near, waiting just around the next bend."

In the center of the labyrinth, I look back into the past: grandchildren at the beach; my dog, Fred, asleep under the tree; my husband, John, absorbed in his workshop. I look ahead to what might be: a walk with John in a golden wood, leaves drifting down on us; a class discussion on an insightful text, Thanksgiving dinner with family, Advent's arrival, and curling up in a blanket on a snowy Christmas Eve near a roaring fire.

I cherish my time in the labyrinth's center, cradled by my past and anticipating my future. I hold the moment loosely, knowing I cannot remain here long.

Stepping out from the center, I open my eyes, my arms, and my heart to the possibilities of a sacred life yet to be. I give my memories permission now to become sources of strength, and I begin to face the ghosts that lie ahead.

~ Ruth Jewell

SEASONING THE SOUL

Shall we note the beauty of the circle?
Shall we praise the curve of spheres?
Together let us witness their sweet perfection.

Onion, papery orb, when cut
reveals its many inner circles
complete and tart.
Drop of water fallen on rock.

It knows its shape, and shows it.
Pomegranate, humble, leathery,
its red and lumpy radius
embraces scarlet secret seeds.

Labyrinth Circle, winding, looping, leading, hiding, flinging us out

and guiding us home.

~ *Sheila Dierks*, excerpted from *A Midweek Meditation*

Photo by Diane Ahern Photography

May the surprises that await you this autumn day
and the days ahead,
not overwhelm,
but rather draw you deeper into the beauty
alive
in the depths of your own soul.

~ Eileen Knoff

Befriended by the Light

May autumn's light,
now subdued,
ease your struggle

as does the presence of an anam cara;
May autumn's glow befriend you
body and soul.

May this light guide you to the Divine Light
Who will be your Anam Cara,
drawing forth your own radiance,
casting shadows that you do not fear
to look upon with understanding

and with gratitude for all that has been
and all that is,
and all that will be

~ *Eileen Knoff*

Autumn and the Anam Cara

Formed from the same clay
Fired in the Kiln of God's love
Two Vessels, one Soul

There is a beauty in autumn that speaks to the Soul. The colors and cooling of this season invite introspection. It is a time of both release and renewal. Release in that the fecund days of summer submit to the harvest; renewal of the rhythms of school and study, home and hearth. It is a fitting time, therefore, to consider the Celtic notion of Anam Cara (Soul Friend).

To have an Anam Cara in one's life is to know both release and renewal. With your Anam Cara, you can release all judgments and attachments. As you release you are, in turn, released. The masks and veils of many lifetimes are dissolved and you are free to love as you have never loved before. In a word, you are renewed. Taste, touch, sights, sounds and smells are all refreshed. You know, truly know, that this soul friend has always been and always will be one with you. As in the sudden understanding of a Zen koan, you now know the true meaning of Celtic design and the circle that is Celtic time.

May all who read these words find your Anam Cara in this life or the next. S/he is waiting.

My Anam Cara
Not one, not two: Trinity
Two vessels, one Soul.

~ *David Garner*

Releasing Autumn

Dropping Down the Well

The Irish countryside abounds with wells—strange and mysterious spaces that entice me to bend over and explore those darker depths I normally avoid.

The symbol of the well came to me in considering an autumn question to put forth to the *Brigid's Circle* subscriber group: What surprises of this past year am I now harvesting in my life? The primary surprise I encountered while reflecting on my past year was the presence of a strange attractor drawing me downward and inward, as if into a well of strength and grace flowing underneath my daily current events. Despite countless ministerial and social commitments, deadlines, trips, house repairs, visits to doctors and dentists, there was yet a gentle force tugging me toward a deeper flow with its Wisdom of letting go.

The pull first presented itself in January with the death of a pastoral colleague, Kate O'Sullivan. An Episcopal chaplain, Kate was a great believer in a mysterious, graceful presence at work in all circumstances. Kate naturally carried that presence to others, especially her patients at Children's Hospital. I experienced Kate's belief expand and intensify just before her learning that she had developed pancreatic cancer.

The cancer claimed her life within a few months. The Episcopal cathedral in Seattle was packed for her funeral with people from all faith traditions. As I read the order of service, I discovered that both Kate and I had been born in 1955. I was struck with the awareness that this could have been me lying there. Instead, I remained here, wondering how to become the kind of presence Kate had been.

Nine months before her death, Kate had noticed my interest in Celtic spirituality and urged me to share its insights with a committee she was chairing on the environment. While preparing my talk, I heard within a call to allow the Earth itself to become an Anam Cara, a soulfriend. I heeded what I heard and shared that message with the group. They responded eagerly!

Since then, I have tried to live into this relationship by letting Nature reveal to me the beauty of "God's original gospel," with its cycles of light and dark, life and death. The more I pay attention to the Wisdom in the Earth the more I am able to drop down into the heart of my life and the challenges within its changing seasons, its daily deaths.

Kate's death was my first important letting go this year. It was not the last. A dear aunt died, older siblings have struggled with serious illnesses, a daughter moved away, and I have had to make difficult decisions that pleased some and displeased others. The year's transitions have called me to grow into new stages of trust in my own experiences and generosity with the gifts I still do have to share. I see now that the grace of Divine Life has been present within each transition and always will be. I need only to risk following the lure of Love, who urges me to bend low and scoop into empty hands the Life-Giving Water that waits patiently in the well of my own soul.

~ *Eileen Knoff*

Photo by Liz Knoff Floodeen

SEASONING THE SOUL

Photo by Liz Knoff Floodeen

May morning mists bathe your lungs that you might breathe deeply.
May morning mists open you to new possibilities wrapped in their cool embrace.
May what is hidden become clear.
May morning mists bring new ways of seeing yourself and The Divine.

~ Beth Beyer Abbott

Autumn's Mist

Window beckons,
need for bearings.
But wait!
Landscape muted
in misty wonder.

What is there,
hidden in Nature's exhale?
Ancient song emerges
out of silence.

I often use my yard as a vehicle for gazing prayer. This thin space opens me to possibilities beyond the rationality of time and space. I've had glimpses of a former life: emerging from woods at dawn, basket filled with healing herbs. I've heard the chant of Native ancestors. I've felt the powerful energy of the Holy as Full Moon turns darkness into midday light. Fox, hedgehog, ravens, bats, deer and all creation speak messages from God. Morning mists remind me that, in the words of Ann Merrill, "Hidden within creation, You are the Heart of everything."

~ Beth Beyer Abbott

SEASONING THE SOUL

Twirling into Tomorrow

A picture of winding vine from Dromatine,
in Ireland's County Down,
landed on my desk the other day
as I was turning over in my mind
how my life had seemed to circle
round itself, time and time again.

I searched within to comprehend how
it could have been
I landed in the here and now.

A choice? a chance? Or just an invitation
to join the dance of life with all
its changing rhythms swinging me to and fro,
around delightful bends

as well as into missteps I could regret;
and yet what can I really do but give my yes,
lean back, take my turn today
and like the vine,
and twirl into tomorrow

    ~ Eileen Knoff

Releasing Autumn

Photo by Anna Hennessy, C.S.B.

SEASONING THE SOUL

A Blessing of Lughnasadh

May we appreciate and give thanks
For all we have planted, watered, and watched!

Even more, may we thank you, O God,
For your hidden hands which worked with ours;

For the beating of your heart that moved our seedlings upward,
Your bringing of days which carried sunshine and water.

Take heart my companions on the journey!
This same Hidden Mover walks with us,
Each step "a planting"; every breath, some growth.

Behold! The sapling is now the tree.
The child . . . the wise.

And all we have worked so hard to bring forth
All that has been lavishly poured out upon us
Is the mixture with which we will bless the world!

~ Scott Jenkins

Come, join the dance around the bonfires. Celebrate!

Some may question speaking of bounty when the nightly news reports on a global recession and mounting unemployment figures. And, yes, many we know—maybe it's you—are struggling in this economic climate. Still, we live in the midst of bounty that reveals itself in numerous ways. It can be found in the eyes of our loved ones, and sometimes in the eyes of the stranger. It is in the faces of the daisies that sway and move to the rhythms of the breeze.

Earlier this summer, a majestic lift-off of a flock of white pelicans caused all within its sight to stop in mid-step and mid-sentence to observe the breathtaking moment. In that instant I felt a rush of energy that stayed with me throughout that day. As I write, I see it again through my mind's eye and am refreshed.

Indeed, bounty is in our midst. That which we appreciate expands. So, let us gather our baskets and jars. Let us prepare to celebrate the harvest!

~ Sharon Taylor

Photo by Barbie Hull Photography

Photo by Kris Jenkins

A Closing Blessing

During this season of rich ripe abundance
I appreciate Beauty's lessons:

To bloom wholly
care-free of impending frost

To dance and sway with gentle breeze,
surrendering to harsh wind, and, yet
standing tall in stillness.

To accept each moment graciously,
To live the Mystery unquestioningly.

~ Sharon Taylor

Autumn Prayer

Thank you, Source of All, for what we are now harvesting in our lives.
We stand grateful for the growth that summer has brought us.

May our eyes remain open to the beauty of the rich colors of autumn—vibrant orange,
rich magenta, yellow gold, and red maple.
And may our hearts welcome the changes being called forth within us.

May we remain aware of our abundance
and be willing to share it with others.

May we be willing to let go, release and move into the unknown.

~ Jane Comerford

SEASONING THE SOUL

Photo by Sheila Dierks

Sealing the Day

I seal this day, reaching back, full
of the wisdom of eye and ear,
of blood and brain,
of soul and spirit
that the last twelve-month circle has gifted.

I seal this day, certain
that loving arms of the all embracing Godde
encircle me and keep me round
as the months do their work.

~ *Sheila Dierks*

A Farewell

As the day's light wanes
may we savor the taste of a year well lived.

May its memories bless us in knowing
we have given our best.

O, Sun, off the coastal west,
grant us our much needed rest.

~ Eileen Knoff

Photo by Anna Hennessy, C.S.B., October 31, 2010, Donegal, Ireland

SEASONING THE SOUL

Questions for Reflection by Individuals or Groups

Jane Comerford's "A Harvest Reflection" invited us to consider the questions below. What do you find yourself aware of as you ponder these questions:

What are the interior fruits that I am harvesting from past plantings?

What gifts of the Spirit has the "wild goose" brought into my life this past summer?

What must I start now to release to be open to the new still ahead of me?

Questions for Reflection

What shifts do you notice in yourself as you move into or through this harvest season? Does anything surprise you?

What are the areas of light and darkness in your life these days? If you let them enter into dialogue with one another and your soul, what do you discover?

What is ending for you now? And what seeds are being planted that you may harvest in the new year?

What is living in you now as a result of having reflected on the seasons with this collection as your companion?

Annotated Bibliography
Celtic Spirituality

Cahill, Thomas. *How the Irish Saved Civilization.* New York: Anchor Books, Doubleday. 1995.
> Highly readable description of Rome's fall, Ireland's early history, Ireland's turn toward Christianity, and then the Christian monks bringing of the ancient learning transcribed by Irish monks back to the continent of Europe during its "dark age." Cahill treats the Irish story as a salvation story of Christianity with early Irish saints as the heroes. He may exaggerate Ireland's role, but he has certainly collected numerous facts to support his thesis, which he tells in a very appealing fashion. He is much stronger on the masculine side of the story than the feminine. For some balance see Meehan's and Oliver's *Praying with Celtic Holy Women* (below) and Rita Minehan's *Rekindling the Flame* (also below).

Carmichael, Alexander, ed. *The Carmina Gadelica.* Six volumes. First published in 1900 with several subsequent editions and publications.
> Carmichael's collection has become a foundational text for understanding the spirit and content of Celtic prayer of the people as distinct from the formal prayers of the Ecclesia. Some critics charge that Carmichael may have taken liberties in his transcriptions; nevertheless his work marks a sizable research study of everyday prayers of the Scottish people that seemed to be vanishing at the turn of the past century. I generally have used the translations found in Esther de Waal's *Celtic Way of Prayer* when I have cited it (see below).

Condren, Mary. *The Serpent and the Goddess: Women Religion, and Power in Celtic Ireland.* San Francisco: Harper Row, 1989.
> A valuable study by a respected feminist Harvard scholar that includes the exploration of Brigid as both goddess and saint in the Celtic mind of the past and the implications for our current era of the goddess archetype she represents.

De Waal, Esther. *The Celtic Way of Prayer: The Recovery of the Religious Imagination.* New York: Image Books, Doubleday. 1997.
> One of my foundational and favorite texts on Celtic spirituality, de Waal has built chapters around core themes including journeying, image and song, the trinity, time, the presence of God, the solitary, dark forces, the cross, the saints, and praise. She is gentle and respectful in her tone, clearly one who cherishes this spirituality and has woven it into her daily life. Reading de Waal serves as a kind of meditation for me that I come back to time and time again. I highly recommend it!

Hennessy, Anna, C.S.B. *Glimpses*. Dublin: Brigidine Community. 2007.
> Personal poems covering the seasons of the year by this sister of St. Brigid residing in Dublin, Ireland.

Meehan, Bridget Mary and Regina Madonna Oliver. *Praying with Celtic Holy Women*. Liguori, Missouri. Liguori/Triumph Imprint, Liguori Publications. 2003.
> Meehan and Oliver have written a delightful work about the legends of Celtic women, many who span both the pre-Christian and Christian Ireland. Rituals connected to these women written by Meehan and Oliver are included. They tell some interesting tales along the way of personal research that included tromping through Irish fields to find legendary wells and hear stories told about favorite local saints by today's residents of that area. I have used a number of their prayer rituals with groups I have led in recent years and found them very fruitful, especially the ritual for Brigid, Hilda, and Tegla. An extensive annotated bibliography concludes the work. Worth having on your shelf. Available on Kindle.

Minehan, Rita. *Rekindling the Flame: A Pilgrimage in the Footsteps of Brigid of Ireland*. Kildare, Ireland: Solas Bhride Community. 1999. Funded by a grant of The Heritage Council.
> A brief, yet full, description of Brigid's place in the Irish story as well as information on taking a pilgrimage through her story in Kildare at Solas Bhride. As with the Meehan and de Waal works, this book also includes a number of lovely prayers. A helpful little compendium for understanding Brigid as both goddess and saint. One of the first books I was given by a sister of St. Brigid to begin to understand her role in the Irish and perhaps the planetary experience.

Newell, J. Phillip. *Christ of the Celts*. San Francisco: Jossey-Bass, A Wiley Imprint. 2008.
> For me, this has been an essential source for Celtic themes of the goodness at the heart of all creation and how Christianity lost that awareness. Some detail about the Pelagian/Augstinian debate. Newell argues persuasively that humanity is being called to reclaim the vision of our essential goodness in our time, a vision Newell believes can be found at the heart of Celtic-Christian spirituality. Newell seems to have shifted the way he was holding the creative tension he speaks of in the book below, written a decade earlier. Newell seems to have made a decision in the last decade to shift his focus toward the Christ that is in all things, letting Christ in the ecclesia fend for himself. Or maybe I'm reading myself into Newell's book?

———*Listening for the Heartbeat of God*. New York: Paulist Press. 1997.
> Similar themes to *Christ of the Celts*, with an emphasis on ways to listen for the goodness in all creation and act upon it. Newell relates types of listening with noted visionaries of

Celtic spiritual history. At the conclusion he contrasts the Celtic (Johannine) and Roman (Petrine) ways of listening to God within everyday life and the life of the church and calls for a creative tension to be held between the two.

O'Donohue, John. *Anam Cara*. New York: Cliff Street Books, a Harper Collins imprint, 1997.
———*Beauty: The Invisible Embrace*. New York: Perennial, a Harper Collins imprint, 2003.
Both of these books, and just about anything else by John O'Donohue, bear reading over and over again. Deep, transformative visions crafted by a master wordsmith. *Anam Cara* is about the soul friendship that is of the essence in Celtic spirituality. It also covers life, death, beauty, and solitude—all wrapped up in a Celtic vision. The second book expands the author's insights into beauty. (The quotation at the beginning of this book's preface can be found on p. 31 of O'Donohue's book.) This became an essential reference for my work as I found myself called more and more to drop into the awareness of beauty as I developed this book. O'Donohue proposes that "much of the stress and emptiness that haunts us can be traced back to our lack of attention to beauty." To O'Donohue beauty is a "possibility that enlarges and delights the heart." All his works do that. I advise having them close at hand. His insights are foundational to what I have done in this project.

O'Duinn, Sean, O.S.B. *The Rites of Brigid, Goddess and Saint*. Dublin: The Columba Press. 2005.
Valuable reference to understand the meaning of Brigid and learn about the many rites surrounding her feast on February 1. Basic background for anyone desiring to understand Brigid.

Woods, Richard. "The Spirituality of the Celtic Church." In *Spirituality Today* (Vol 37: No. 3, pp. 243-55, 1985). Also online at http://www.spiritualitytoday.org/spir2day/853735woods.html.

On Mysticism, Creation-Centered Spirituality, and the Emerging Paradigm

Bear and Company, Rochester Vermont, Centering Series. 1983.
———*Meditations with Hildegard von Bingen* (ed. Gabriele Uhlein).
———*Meditations with Julian of Norwich* (ed. Brendan Doyle).
———*Meditations with Meister Eckhart* (ed. Matthew Fox).
———*Meditations with Teilhard de Chardin* (ed. Blanche Gallagher).
Reflecting with these mystics is both inspiring and helpful in seeing how the ancient and the new are in ongoing conversation in our times.

Cannato, Judy. *Radical Amazement: Contemplative Lessons from Black Holes, Supernovas, and other Wonders of the Universe*, Notre Dame, Indiana. Soren Books, 2006.

Fox, Matthew. *One River, Many Wells*. New York: Penguin Putnam, Inc., 2000.
> Matt Fox has been very prolific in teaching, writing, speaking about, and celebrating the New Cosmic Story/Creation-Centered Spirituality. This is only one of many possible sources by Fox, but it is one I have turned to often for reminders of the way Wisdom is present in such diversity and beauty. The chapters here invite readers to consider how humanity has been relating to creation, divinity, ourselves and what that means for the future.

O'Murchu, Diarmud. *Evolutionary Faith*. New York: Orbis Books, 2002.
——*Quantum Theology: Spiritual Implications of the New Physics*. Crossroad Publishing, 2nd Printing, 2000.
——*Religion in Exile: A Spiritual Homecoming*. Crossroad Publishing Co., 2000.
> Essential background to the changing paradigms in which we are living.

Phillips, Jan. *No Ordinary Time: The Rise of Spiritual Intelligence and Evolutionary Creativity*. San Diego: Livingkindness Foundation, 2011.
> Written as a Divine Office for our age of evolutionary spiritual awakening, Jan offers the user a daily diet of insights for becoming the humanity we are meant to be. I return to this book often for reflection and spiritual energizing. (The quotation on p. 37 of this book can be found on p. 19 of Jan's book.)

Morwood, Michael. *From Sand to Solid Ground*. New York: Crossroad Publishing, 2007.
——*Praying a New Story*. New York: Orbis Books. 2004.
> Morwood's insights and prayer language have helped me embody emerging paradigms in prayer. He is a helpful bridge from the past to the possible future.

Wessels, Cletus. *Jesus in the New Universe Story*. New York: Orbis Books, 2003.
> Wessels reinterprets traditional concepts for an evolutionary age. He constructs a model for understanding humanity's evolution, breaking it into three periods: childhood, adolescence, and adulthood.

Many other sources can be uncovered on these and other related themes by these and other authors to whom their reference lists can lead you. I have offered them since I often referred to each of them, and they may provide you a jumping-off point to your own exploration of Celtic spirituality.

Acknowledgments

It has taken a whole host of dedicated and caring contributors to bring this book to birth. First, I offer my deep thanks to the four ministerial colleagues with the Ecumenical Catholic Communion whose round-robin emails with me were the seeds for the monthly Brigid's Circle publication that eventually became this book. They include Rev. Scott Jenkins (Colorado), Rev. Kedda Keough (Washington), Rev. Kathy McCarthy (California) and Spiritual Director Sharon Taylor (Colorado). Thank you all for your willingness to explore this spirituality with me online and to open our emails to a wider audience. Kathy, thank you for the opportunity to offer a Celtic workshop at the Pathfinder community in Bermuda Dunes, and to include a picture of that community in this book.

I am grateful to the first few photographers and contributors who joined the five of us in those early years: David Garner, Anna Hennessy, Barbie Hull and Kris Jenkins. Your generous spirits set the tone of this project. Thank you, Diane Ahern and Liz Floodeen for adding your photos to the sequence in later years, and then agreeing to include them in this book.

The contributors, who are listed in the index that follows these acknowledgments , have made this book possible. Each has looked closely, listened attentive, dug deeply, and responded creatively to find the words and images that comprise this book. Despite full schedules and busy lives, they have met deadlines graciously. I am grateful for you all!

An additional word of thanks to contributor Sharon Taylor, who wrote early and often for the monthly publication which was the source for the material in this book. Sharon also helped lay out the monthly sequence for several months. When Sharon could no longer tend to the layout, Rev. Mandy Bennett, then a communications coordinator for Claremont College and later a priest with the Ecumenical Catholic Communion, came to my aid. Soon thereafter Mandy began to offer her writings to the monthly publication. Thank you, Mandy, for your support as well.

Behind the Scenes

In addition to the contributors whose work you see here there are some important behind-the-scenes people who deserve mention. Foremost among them are the page designers and print managers who assisted me in bringing this book to press. Vicki McVey in Colorado helped me envision the basic layout design through the first season with the support of Sheila Dierks of WovenWord Press. Sheila is also a writer and photographer for this collection. Thank you, Sheila, for your support in the early stages of this book and your wonderful written and photographic contributions. Stacy Montgomery, principal of Stacy Montgomery Designer, in Seattle, helped solidify the layout further, taking it through all four seasons.

Judith Jones of Pilgrim Spirit Communications came on to finish the layout work for the first edition and has overseen all aspects of bringing this book to publication. She has been of inestimable help in all technical areas, and many emotional ones too. I would not have made it to press without your faithful and expert support nor would we now have this second edition of the book.

Spiritual support

Many thanks to Dr. Bridget Mary Meehan, leader of the Association of Roman Catholic Woman Priests and dean of my doctoral program of studies at Global Ministries University. I very much needed her unwavering encouragement and steady belief in my abilities and in the work itself. I valued her insistence that I finish the work when I began to doubt my ability to do so.

I thank Sr. Jane Comerford for inviting me to go on pilgrimage to Ireland, where my emerging interest in Celtic spirituality took root in 2007; also appreciation to Seattle University's Pastoral Leadership Program directors and mentors Dr. Marianne LaBarre, Rev. Dr. Suzanne Seaton, and Dr. Valerie Lesniak, who have steadily encouraged me along the way of this journey into Celtic spirituality and supported my desire to bring my efforts into book publication.

I appreciate the support of WomanSpirit Center's co-director Evelyn Wemhoff for opening your space and heart to my sharing of this spirituality for several years, as well as serving as my personal spiritual director for the good part of a decade. Leaders of the Ecumenical Communion in the presiding bishops' office—Chancellor George von Stamwitz and Presiding Bishop Peter Hickman—provided ongoing encouragement to me and to Brigid's Circle in its early days, welcoming the ministry into the communion and subscribing personally to monthly publication. I appreciate your vote of confidence in our efforts.

Many members of the Roman Catholic Woman Priest movement encouraged me in the Celtic spiritual ministry, especially Rev. Diane Whalen, Rev. Sandi DeMaster, and the West Coast Roman Catholic Woman Priest Bishop Olivia Doko. Rev. Victoria Rue and Rev. Mary Ellen Robinson, thank you. for your contributions to this collection and for all you are doing to bring greater justice into the Roman Catholic Church and the world at large.

To Rev. Dr. Mary Theresa Streck, a leader in the Association of Roman Catholic Women Priests, thank you for your desire to share parts of the first edition with members of your community. Disciples of Christ pastor Rev. Kara Markell, thank you for inviting me to share this work with members of your community in workshops both locally and regionally. Thank you to all reviewers of the first edition who have seen value in this work and encouraged others to see it too.

A special note of thanks to Roger McClellan, a founding leader of the Progressive Christian Alliance. You were a light in the darkness to me and my ministry. Thank you for your inclusive vision and for your encouragement of my ordination and for contributing to Brigid's Circle!

Acknowledgments

And finally I thank my husband Stephen who bears with me through all the ups and downs of my writing, editing, and publishing. For your emotional—and financial—support, I offer thanks from the bottom of my heart!

Index of Contributors

Beth Beyer Abbott 105, 106, 107

Diane Ahern 11, 12, 93, 101

Mandy Bennett 79, 81

Cheryl Anne 8, 38, 44, 54, 82, 86

William Clyma 21

Jane Comerford 32, 37, 90, 95, 113

Michelle Conklin 14

Sheila Dierks 13, 15, 28, 45, 46, 100, 114

Liz Knoff Floodeen 33, 60, 97, 105, 106

David Garner 34, 36, 71, 91, 94, 103

Anna Hennessy 43, 92, 96, 109, 115

Barbie Hull 7, 8, 18, 19, 24, 26, 27, 34, 39, 40, 48, 65, 80, 81, 86, 90, 95, 111

Kris Jenkins 41, 84, 94, 98, 112

Scott Jenkins 10, 62, 63, 110

Ruth Jewell 99

Kedda Keough 49, 52, 98

Eileen Knoff 7, 10, 12, 14, 18, 21, 23, 25, 26, 27, 36, 37, 40, 42, 46, 47, 48, 50, 51, 53, 54, 55, 56, 62, 64, 66, 67, 68, 72, 75, 76, 96, 97, 99, 101, 102, 105, 108, 115

Mary Kay Krause 15

Kathy McCarthy 19

Roger McClellan 65, 74

Jan Phillips 1, 35

Denise Pyles 17, 66, 73

Mary Ellen Robertson 52

Victoria Rue 24, 28

Sharon Taylor 6, 13, 18, 20, 39, 52, 83, 85, 92, 111, 112

Contact information for the contributors to this collection may be found online or by contacting the editor.

Correspondence for the editor, Eileen Knoff, D.Min., should be addressed to eileenknoff@yahoo.com.

This book was brought to publishing with the assistance of Judith Jones at Pilgrim Spirit Communications.

Contact Judith via judith@pilgrimspirit.com or see www.pilgrimspirit.com.